I0201596

King Charles III

Leslie Buffam

Explore other books at:
WWW.ENGAGEBOOKS.COM

VANCOUVER, B.C.

WWW.ENGAGEBOOKS.COM

King Charles III: Level 2
Remarkable People
Leslie Buffam 1949 –
Text © 2024 Engage Books
Design © 2024 Engage Books

Edited by: A.R. Roumanis, Melody Sun,
Ashley Lee & Sarah Harvey
Design by: Rose Gowsell Pattison

Text set in Arial Regular.
Chapter headings set in Arial Black.

FIRST EDITION / FIRST PRINTING

LIBRARY AND ARCHIVES CANADA CATALOGUING IN PUBLICATION

Title: King Charles III: Remarkable People / Leslie Buffam
Names: Buffam, Leslie, 1949- author

Identifiers: Canadiana (print) 20200308874 | Canadiana (ebook) 20200308912
ISBN 978-1-77878-190-2 (hardcover)
ISBN 978-1-77878-191-9 (softcover)
ISBN 978-1-77878-193-3 (pdf)
ISBN 978-1-77878-192-6 (epub)
ISBN 978-1-77878-194-0 (audio)

Subjects:
LCSH: Biographies—Juvenile literature

Classification: SF426.5 .L44 20200 | DDC J636.7—DC23

This project has been made possible in part
by the Government of Canada.

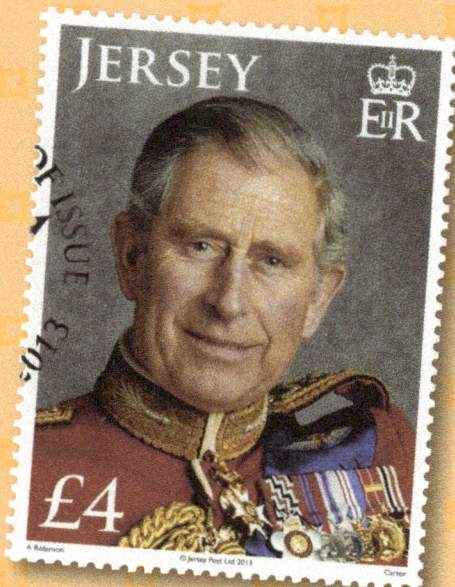

Canada

Contents

Who Is King Charles III?

King Charles III is the King of the United Kingdom. He is also King of the **Commonwealth of Nations**. He became King on September 8, 2022.

The United Kingdom includes England, Scotland, Wales, and Northern Ireland.

KEY WORD

Commonwealth of Nations: a group of more than 50 countries.

Prince Charles was 73 years old when he became King. His mother, Queen Elizabeth II, had **reigned** for almost 71 years.

KEY WORD

Reigned: ruled.

Early Life

Prince Charles was born at Buckingham Palace on November 14, 1948. His parents were Princess Elizabeth and Prince Philip, Duke of Edinburgh.

Prince Charles's world changed in February, 1952. His mother became Queen Elizabeth II. His parents were often gone for months at a time on Royal tours. Prince Charles and his little sister, Princess Anne, stayed home.

Prince Charles and Princess Anne have always been very close.

Education

Prince Charles began school at home. He started **boarding school** in England at age 8. At 13, he was sent to a Scottish boarding school. His father had gone to the same school.

KEY WORD

Boarding school: a school where students live during the school terms.

At boarding school, Prince Charles studied drama, history, Latin, and French. He played a Pirate King in one of the school's plays. He was **head boy** in his final year of school.

9

Britain During The King's Childhood

Prince Charles was a young boy during the 1950s. **Britons** were still recovering from World War II. There was not enough food and housing.

KEY WORD

Britons: people who live in Great Britain.

In the 1960s, televisions and refrigerators made home life better. Food **rationing** was no longer needed. Many new homes were being built. British pop music took the world by storm.

The Beatles played for members of the Royal Family in 1963.

KEY WORD

Rationing: limiting the amount of something.

From Student to Officer

Prince Charles went to Cambridge University after he left boarding school. He was the first heir to the British throne to attend university and get a degree.

Prince Charles got a degree in history in 1970.

Prince Charles spoke Welsh at the ceremony where he became the Prince of Wales.

In 1969, Prince Charles spent one term at a Welsh university. A special tutor helped him learn to speak Welsh. Later that year, Prince Charles was crowned the Prince of Wales.

Prince Charles at Work

When Prince Charles became the Prince of Wales, he became the official heir to the throne. He began to take on some Royal duties.

Prince Charles's father, grandfather, and great-grandfather all served in the British Royal Navy.

Prince Charles attended the Royal Air Force College. He became a pilot. He also served in the Royal Navy.

Influences and Interests

Prince Charles started watercolor painting at boarding school. He loves landscape painting. He gives all of the money from the sales of his paintings to charities.

Helping others is important to Prince Charles. In 1976, he set up the Prince's Trust. One of its goals is to help young people get their lives on track.

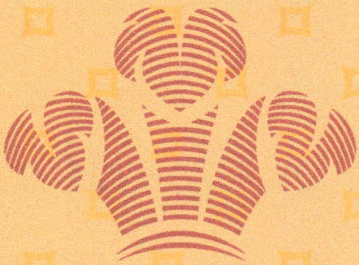

Prince's Trust

The Prince's Trust has helped more than 1 million young people to find careers and start businesses.

Personal Life

Prince Charles grew up in Buckingham Palace. He often spent summers at Balmoral Castle in Scotland. He was particularly happy outdoors.

Prince Charles taught his children to fly fish at Balmoral when they were little boys.

1999

Prince Charles & Lady
Diana Spencer

KOMI

5,00

750 million people watched
the Royal Wedding on TV.

On July 29, 1981, Prince Charles
married Lady Diana Spencer.
Their two children are Prince
William and Prince Harry.
Prince Charles and Lady Diana
separated in 1993.

Legacy as Prince of Wales

Prince Charles gives his time and energy to important causes. He is interested in saving old buildings and teaching art to children. His desire to help others is part of his **legacy**.

KEY WORD

Legacy: something that is passed on to future generations.

Prince Charles often speaks out about climate change. He is passionate about environmental issues. One of the goals of the Prince's Trust is to make **sustainability** a reality.

KEY WORD

Sustainability: the balance between resource use and care for the environment.

Becoming King Charles III

Prince Charles took on more Royal duties as his mother got older. His father, Prince Philip, died in 2021, aged 99. His mother died on September 8, 2022, aged 96. Prince Charles became King Charles III.

Every **monarch** has a different approach to being king or queen. King Charles III wants to be actively involved in making positive changes in the world.

KEY WORD

Monarch: someone who reigns for life.

IT'S TRUE!

Facts About King Charles III

Prince Charles starred as Macbeth while at boarding school.

In 2005, Prince Charles married Camilla Parker-Bowles. She is now The Queen.

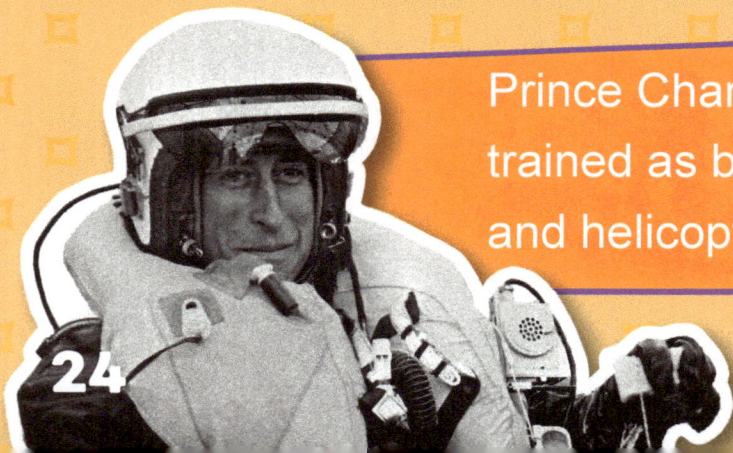

Prince Charles trained as both a jet and helicopter pilot.

Prince Charles has set up more than 25 charities in 40 years.

The Prince's Trust helped start Idris Elba's acting career.

Prince Charles wrote a book called *The Old Man of Lochnagar.*

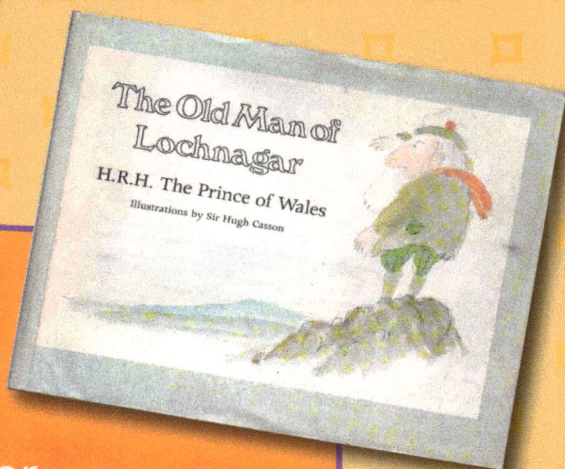

The Old Man of Lochnagar

H.R.H. The Prince of Wales

Illustrations by Sir Hugh Casson

TIMELINE

November 14, 1948
Prince Charles
is born

February 6, 1952
his mother becomes
Queen Elizabeth II

July 1969
crowned the
Prince of Wales

1970
graduates from
university

July 29, 1981
marries Lady Diana
Spencer

June 21, 1982
Prince William
is born

August 31, 1997
Princess Diana dies in
a car crash in France

April 9, 2005
marries Camilla
Parker-Bowles

April 1962-1967 attends his father's old boarding school

October 1967 goes to university

1971-1976 serves in the Royal Air Force and then the Royal Navy

1976 leaves the navy and starts the Prince's Trust charity

September 15, 1984 Prince Harry is born

December 9, 1993 separates from Diana

May 10, 2022 Prince Charles stands in for Queen Elizabeth II at the state opening of Parliament

September 8, 2022 Queen Elizabeth II dies. Prince Charles becomes King Charles III.

Be Like King Charles III

If you would like to be like King Charles III

- Do what you can to help those less fortunate than you.
- Understand your strengths. Make the most of them.
- Find pleasure in simple things.

- Spend time with those who mean the most to you.

- Keep a good sense of humor.

Quiz

Test your knowledge of King Charles III by answering the following questions. The questions are based on what you have read in this book. The answers are listed on the bottom of the next page.

1 How old was Prince Charles when he became King?

2 What did a special tutor help Prince Charles learn at university?

3 What degree did Prince Charles get in 1970?

4 What did Prince Charles set up to help young people get their lives on track?

5 Who did Prince Charles star as while at boarding school?

6 Who did Prince Charles marry in 2005?

Explore other Readers.

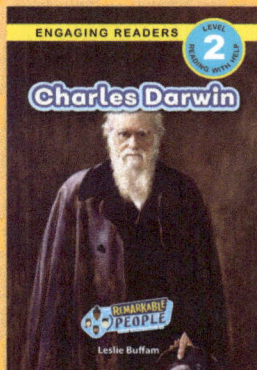

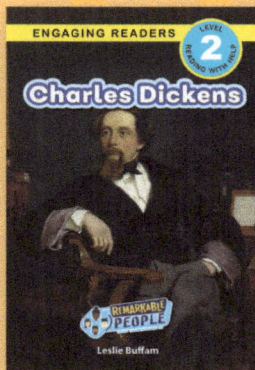

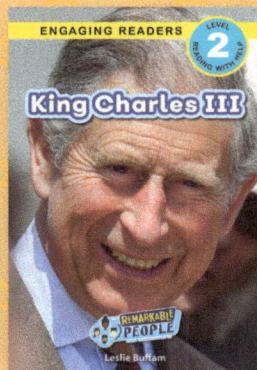

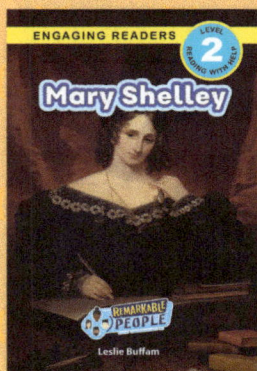

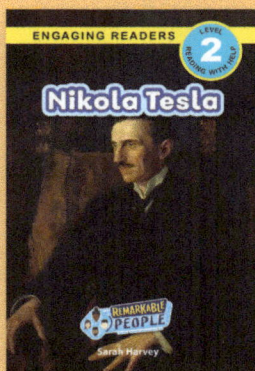

Visit www.engagebooks.com/readers

Answers: 1. 73 2. The Welsh language 3. A history degree 4. The Prince's Trust 5. Macbeth 6. Camilla Parker-Bowles